THE
GRATITUDE
JOURNAL

This journal belongs to:

_____

POTTER

"Acknowledging the good that you already have in your life is the foundation for all abundance." —ECKHART TOLLE

—————————

What is a gratitude journal? It's a place to record the things you're most grateful for, from the serendipitous moments that spark joy and the people who touch your heart to the simple—even mundane—pleasures of everyday life.

Why use one? Because gratitude is literally good for your health. Research shows that engaging in a regular gratitude practice counterbalances the negativity we inevitably experience in our lives; gratitude begets more gratitude. Journaling has proven to have tangible physical benefits too, including lowered stress levels, better sleep, and more motivation for regular exercise.

How do you use this journal? Simply jot down three things you are grateful for each day. There is enough space here to capture short gratitude lists for three years. Perhaps you start your day with a list; perhaps you end your day with one. There is no wrong way to use this journal.

—————————

Here are two important things to remember:
Pay attention!
Cultivating a regular gratitude practice starts with mindfulness. You might have to practice checking in with yourself every day before it becomes an effortless part of your routine.

Be specific!
When you flip back through your journal, the details of days past are more likely to fill you up with warmth than simple descriptions like "music" or "the weather." Capture the specifics, so that when you look back, you'll see just how much abundance you already have.

Here's to three years of gratitude. Happy journaling.

JANUARY 1

20_____

1. _____
_____
2. _____
_____
3. _____
_____

20_____

1. _____
_____
2. _____
_____
3. _____
_____

20_____

1. _____
_____
2. _____
_____
3. _____
_____

JANUARY 2

20_____

   1. _____

   _____

   2. _____

   _____

   3. _____

   _____

20_____

   1. _____

   _____

   2. _____

   _____

   3. _____

   _____

20_____

   1. _____

   _____

   2. _____

   _____

   3. _____

   _____

JANUARY 3

20_____

   1. _____

     _____

   2. _____

     _____

   3. _____

     _____

20_____

   1. _____

     _____

   2. _____

     _____

   3. _____

     _____

20_____

   1. _____

     _____

   2. _____

     _____

   3. _____

     _____

JANUARY 4

20_____

1. _____
_____
2. _____
_____
3. _____
_____

20_____

1. _____
_____
2. _____
_____
3. _____
_____

20_____

1. _____
_____
2. _____
_____
3. _____
_____

JANUARY 5

20_____

1. _____

_____

2. _____

_____

3. _____

_____

20_____

1. _____

_____

2. _____

_____

3. _____

_____

20_____

1. _____

_____

2. _____

_____

3. _____

_____

JANUARY 6

20_____

1. _____
   _____
2. _____
   _____
3. _____
   _____

20_____

1. _____
   _____
2. _____
   _____
3. _____
   _____

20_____

1. _____
   _____
2. _____
   _____
3. _____
   _____

JANUARY 7

20_____

1. _____
   _____
2. _____
   _____
3. _____
   _____

20_____

1. _____
   _____
2. _____
   _____
3. _____
   _____

20_____

1. _____
   _____
2. _____
   _____
3. _____
   _____

JANUARY 8

20_____

   1. _____

     _____

   2. _____

     _____

   3. _____

     _____

20_____

   1. _____

     _____

   2. _____

     _____

   3. _____

     _____

20_____

   1. _____

     _____

   2. _____

     _____

   3. _____

     _____

JANUARY 9

20_____

1. _____
   _____
2. _____
   _____
3. _____
   _____

20_____

1. _____
   _____
2. _____
   _____
3. _____
   _____

20_____

1. _____
   _____
2. _____
   _____
3. _____
   _____

JANUARY 10

20_____

1. _____
   _____

2. _____
   _____

3. _____
   _____

20_____

1. _____
   _____

2. _____
   _____

3. _____
   _____

20_____

1. _____
   _____

2. _____
   _____

3. _____
   _____

JANUARY 11

20_____

   1. _____

     _____

   2. _____

     _____

   3. _____

     _____

20_____

   1. _____

     _____

   2. _____

     _____

   3. _____

     _____

20_____

   1. _____

     _____

   2. _____

     _____

   3. _____

     _____

JANUARY 12

20_____

   1. _____

     _____

   2. _____

     _____

   3. _____

     _____

20_____

   1. _____

     _____

   2. _____

     _____

   3. _____

     _____

20_____

   1. _____

     _____

   2. _____

     _____

   3. _____

     _____

JANUARY 13

20_____

    1. _____

    _____

    2. _____

    _____

    3. _____

    _____

20_____

    1. _____

    _____

    2. _____

    _____

    3. _____

    _____

20_____

    1. _____

    _____

    2. _____

    _____

    3. _____

    _____

JANUARY 14

20_____

    1. _____

      _____

    2. _____

      _____

    3. _____

      _____

20_____

    1. _____

      _____

    2. _____

      _____

    3. _____

      _____

20_____

    1. _____

      _____

    2. _____

      _____

    3. _____

      _____

JANUARY 15

20_____

1. _____

_____

2. _____

_____

3. _____

_____

20_____

1. _____

_____

2. _____

_____

3. _____

_____

20_____

1. _____

_____

2. _____

_____

3. _____

_____

JANUARY 16

20_____

1. _____
   _____
2. _____
   _____
3. _____
   _____

20_____

1. _____
   _____
2. _____
   _____
3. _____
   _____

20_____

1. _____
   _____
2. _____
   _____
3. _____
   _____

JANUARY 17

20_____

   1. _____

      _____

   2. _____

      _____

   3. _____

      _____

20_____

   1. _____

      _____

   2. _____

      _____

   3. _____

      _____

20_____

   1. _____

      _____

   2. _____

      _____

   3. _____

      _____

JANUARY 18

20_____

    1. _____

    _____

    2. _____

    _____

    3. _____

    _____

20_____

    1. _____

    _____

    2. _____

    _____

    3. _____

    _____

20_____

    1. _____

    _____

    2. _____

    _____

    3. _____

    _____

JANUARY 19

20_____

   1. _____

     _____

   2. _____

     _____

   3. _____

     _____

20_____

   1. _____

     _____

   2. _____

     _____

   3. _____

     _____

20_____

   1. _____

     _____

   2. _____

     _____

   3. _____

     _____

JANUARY 20

20_____

1. _____
   _____

2. _____
   _____

3. _____
   _____

20_____

1. _____
   _____

2. _____
   _____

3. _____
   _____

20_____

1. _____
   _____

2. _____
   _____

3. _____
   _____

JANUARY 21

20_____

   1. _____

      _____

   2. _____

      _____

   3. _____

      _____

20_____

   1. _____

      _____

   2. _____

      _____

   3. _____

      _____

20_____

   1. _____

      _____

   2. _____

      _____

   3. _____

      _____

JANUARY 22

20_____

    1. _____

    _____

    2. _____

    _____

    3. _____

    _____

20_____

    1. _____

    _____

    2. _____

    _____

    3. _____

    _____

20_____

    1. _____

    _____

    2. _____

    _____

    3. _____

    _____

JANUARY 23

20_____

1. _____

_____

2. _____

_____

3. _____

_____

20_____

1. _____

_____

2. _____

_____

3. _____

_____

20_____

1. _____

_____

2. _____

_____

3. _____

_____

JANUARY 24

20_____

   1. _____
_____

   2. _____
_____

   3. _____
_____

20_____

   1. _____
_____

   2. _____
_____

   3. _____
_____

20_____

   1. _____
_____

   2. _____
_____

   3. _____
_____

JANUARY 25

20_____

   1. _____

      _____

   2. _____

      _____

   3. _____

      _____

20_____

   1. _____

      _____

   2. _____

      _____

   3. _____

      _____

20_____

   1. _____

      _____

   2. _____

      _____

   3. _____

      _____

JANUARY 26

20_____

1. _____
_____

2. _____
_____

3. _____
_____

20_____

1. _____
_____

2. _____
_____

3. _____
_____

20_____

1. _____
_____

2. _____
_____

3. _____
_____

JANUARY 27

20_____

   1. _____

     _____

   2. _____

     _____

   3. _____

     _____

20_____

   1. _____

     _____

   2. _____

     _____

   3. _____

     _____

20_____

   1. _____

     _____

   2. _____

     _____

   3. _____

     _____

JANUARY 28

20_____

    1. _____

    _____

    2. _____

    _____

    3. _____

    _____

20_____

    1. _____

    _____

    2. _____

    _____

    3. _____

    _____

20_____

    1. _____

    _____

    2. _____

    _____

    3. _____

    _____

JANUARY 29

20_____

   1. _____
    _____

   2. _____
    _____

   3. _____
    _____

20_____

   1. _____
    _____

   2. _____
    _____

   3. _____
    _____

20_____

   1. _____
    _____

   2. _____
    _____

   3. _____
    _____

JANUARY 30

20_____

1. _____

_____

2. _____

_____

3. _____

_____

20_____

1. _____

_____

2. _____

_____

3. _____

_____

20_____

1. _____

_____

2. _____

_____

3. _____

_____

JANUARY 31

20_____

1. _____

_____

2. _____

_____

3. _____

_____

20_____

1. _____

_____

2. _____

_____

3. _____

_____

20_____

1. _____

_____

2. _____

_____

3. _____

_____

FEBRUARY 1

20_____

1. _____
   _____
2. _____
   _____
3. _____
   _____

20_____

1. _____
   _____
2. _____
   _____
3. _____
   _____

20_____

1. _____
   _____
2. _____
   _____
3. _____
   _____

FEBRUARY 2

20____

1. _____

_____

2. _____

_____

3. _____

_____

20____

1. _____

_____

2. _____

_____

3. _____

_____

20____

1. _____

_____

2. _____

_____

3. _____

_____

FEBRUARY 3

20_____

1. _____
_____

2. _____
_____

3. _____
_____

20_____

1. _____
_____

2. _____
_____

3. _____
_____

20_____

1. _____
_____

2. _____
_____

3. _____
_____

FEBRUARY 4

0_____

1. _____

   _____

2. _____

   _____

3. _____

   _____

20_____

1. _____

   _____

2. _____

   _____

3. _____

   _____

20_____

1. _____

   _____

2. _____

   _____

3. _____

   _____

FEBRUARY 5

20_____

   1. _____

     _____

   2. _____

     _____

   3. _____

     _____

20_____

   1. _____

     _____

   2. _____

     _____

   3. _____

     _____

20_____

   1. _____

     _____

   2. _____

     _____

   3. _____

     _____

FEBRUARY 6

20_____

1. _____
   _____
2. _____
   _____
3. _____
   _____

20_____

1. _____
   _____
2. _____
   _____
3. _____
   _____

20_____

1. _____
   _____
2. _____
   _____
3. _____
   _____

FEBRUARY 7

20_____

1. _____
   _____
2. _____
   _____
3. _____
   _____

20_____

1. _____
   _____
2. _____
   _____
3. _____
   _____

20_____

1. _____
   _____
2. _____
   _____
3. _____
   _____

FEBRUARY 8

20_____

1. _____
   _____
2. _____
   _____
3. _____
   _____

20_____

1. _____
   _____
2. _____
   _____
3. _____
   _____

20_____

1. _____
   _____
2. _____
   _____
3. _____
   _____

FEBRUARY 9

20_____

1. _____
_____
2. _____
_____
3. _____
_____

20_____

1. _____
_____
2. _____
_____
3. _____
_____

20_____

1. _____
_____
2. _____
_____
3. _____
_____

FEBRUARY 10

20_____

1. _____
   _____
2. _____
   _____
3. _____
   _____

20_____

1. _____
   _____
2. _____
   _____
3. _____
   _____

20_____

1. _____
   _____
2. _____
   _____
3. _____
   _____

FEBRUARY 11

20_____

1. _____
   _____
2. _____
   _____
3. _____
   _____

20_____

1. _____
   _____
2. _____
   _____
3. _____
   _____

20_____

1. _____
   _____
2. _____
   _____
3. _____
   _____

FEBRUARY 12

20_____

1. _____

_____

2. _____

_____

3. _____

_____

20_____

1. _____

_____

2. _____

_____

3. _____

_____

20_____

1. _____

_____

2. _____

_____

3. _____

_____

FEBRUARY 13

20_____

   1. _____

     _____

   2. _____

     _____

   3. _____

     _____

20_____

   1. _____

     _____

   2. _____

     _____

   3. _____

     _____

20_____

   1. _____

     _____

   2. _____

     _____

   3. _____

     _____

FEBRUARY 14

20_____

1. _____

_____

2. _____

_____

3. _____

_____

20_____

1. _____

_____

2. _____

_____

3. _____

_____

20_____

1. _____

_____

2. _____

_____

3. _____

_____

FEBRUARY 15

20_____

1. _____
_____

2. _____
_____

3. _____
_____

20_____

1. _____
_____

2. _____
_____

3. _____
_____

20_____

1. _____
_____

2. _____
_____

3. _____
_____

FEBRUARY 16

20_____

1. _____
   _____

2. _____
   _____

3. _____
   _____

20_____

1. _____
   _____

2. _____
   _____

3. _____
   _____

20_____

1. _____
   _____

2. _____
   _____

3. _____
   _____

FEBRUARY 17

20_____

1. _____

_____

2. _____

_____

3. _____

_____

20_____

1. _____

_____

2. _____

_____

3. _____

_____

20_____

1. _____

_____

2. _____

_____

3. _____

_____

FEBRUARY 18

20_____

1. _____

_____

2. _____

_____

3. _____

_____

20_____

1. _____

_____

2. _____

_____

3. _____

_____

20_____

1. _____

_____

2. _____

_____

3. _____

_____

FEBRUARY 19

20_____

1. _____
_____

2. _____
_____

3. _____
_____

20_____

1. _____
_____

2. _____
_____

3. _____
_____

20_____

1. _____
_____

2. _____
_____

3. _____
_____

FEBRUARY 20

20_____

   1. _____

   _____

   2. _____

   _____

   3. _____

   _____

20_____

   1. _____

   _____

   2. _____

   _____

   3. _____

   _____

20_____

   1. _____

   _____

   2. _____

   _____

   3. _____

   _____

FEBRUARY 21

20_____

1. _____
   _____
2. _____
   _____
3. _____
   _____

20_____

1. _____
   _____
2. _____
   _____
3. _____
   _____

20_____

1. _____
   _____
2. _____
   _____
3. _____
   _____

FEBRUARY 22

20_____

1. _____
   _____

2. _____
   _____

3. _____
   _____

20_____

1. _____
   _____

2. _____
   _____

3. _____
   _____

20_____

1. _____
   _____

2. _____
   _____

3. _____
   _____

FEBRUARY 23

20_____

1. _____

_____

2. _____

_____

3. _____

_____

20_____

1. _____

_____

2. _____

_____

3. _____

_____

20_____

1. _____

_____

2. _____

_____

3. _____

_____

FEBRUARY 24

20_____

1. _____

_____

2. _____

_____

3. _____

_____

20_____

1. _____

_____

2. _____

_____

3. _____

_____

20_____

1. _____

_____

2. _____

_____

3. _____

_____

FEBRUARY 25

20_____

1. _____
   _____
2. _____
   _____
3. _____
   _____

20_____

1. _____
   _____
2. _____
   _____
3. _____
   _____

20_____

1. _____
   _____
2. _____
   _____
3. _____
   _____

FEBRUARY 26

20_____

1. _____
   _____
2. _____
   _____
3. _____
   _____

20_____

1. _____
   _____
2. _____
   _____
3. _____
   _____

20_____

1. _____
   _____
2. _____
   _____
3. _____
   _____

FEBRUARY 27

20_____

1. _____
_____

2. _____
_____

3. _____
_____

20_____

1. _____
_____

2. _____
_____

3. _____
_____

20_____

1. _____
_____

2. _____
_____

3. _____
_____

FEBRUARY 28

0_____

1. _____
   _____
2. _____
   _____
3. _____
   _____

0_____

1. _____
   _____
2. _____
   _____
3. _____
   _____

0_____

1. _____
   _____
2. _____
   _____
3. _____
   _____

MARCH 1

20_____

   1. _____

     _____

   2. _____

     _____

   3. _____

     _____

20_____

   1. _____

     _____

   2. _____

     _____

   3. _____

     _____

20_____

   1. _____

     _____

   2. _____

     _____

   3. _____

     _____

⊃ _____

1. _____
   _____
2. _____
   _____
3. _____
   _____

⊃ _____

1. _____
   _____
2. _____
   _____
3. _____
   _____

⊃ _____

1. _____
   _____
2. _____
   _____
3. _____
   _____

MARCH 3

20_____

    1. _____

    _____

    2. _____

    _____

    3. _____

    _____

20_____

    1. _____

    _____

    2. _____

    _____

    3. _____

    _____

20_____

    1. _____

    _____

    2. _____

    _____

    3. _____

    _____

MARCH 4

20 _____

1. _____

   _____

2. _____

   _____

3. _____

   _____

20 _____

1. _____

   _____

2. _____

   _____

3. _____

   _____

20 _____

1. _____

   _____

2. _____

   _____

3. _____

   _____

MARCH 5

20_____

    1. _____

    _____

    2. _____

    _____

    3. _____

    _____

20_____

    1. _____

    _____

    2. _____

    _____

    3. _____

    _____

20_____

    1. _____

    _____

    2. _____

    _____

    3. _____

    _____

MARCH 6

20_____

1. _____

_____

2. _____

_____

3. _____

_____

20_____

1. _____

_____

2. _____

_____

3. _____

_____

20_____

1. _____

_____

2. _____

_____

3. _____

_____

MARCH 7

20_____

    1. _____

    _____

    2. _____

    _____

    3. _____

    _____

20_____

    1. _____

    _____

    2. _____

    _____

    3. _____

    _____

20_____

    1. _____

    _____

    2. _____

    _____

    3. _____

    _____

MARCH 8

0 _____

1. _____

_____

2. _____

_____

3. _____

_____

0 _____

1. _____

_____

2. _____

_____

3. _____

_____

0 _____

1. _____

_____

2. _____

_____

3. _____

_____

MARCH 9

20_____

    1. _____

    _____

    2. _____

    _____

    3. _____

    _____

20_____

    1. _____

    _____

    2. _____

    _____

    3. _____

    _____

20_____

    1. _____

    _____

    2. _____

    _____

    3. _____

    _____

MARCH 10

0_____

1. _____

   _____

2. _____

   _____

3. _____

   _____

0_____

1. _____

   _____

2. _____

   _____

3. _____

   _____

0_____

1. _____

   _____

2. _____

   _____

3. _____

   _____

MARCH 11

20_____

    1. _____

       _____

    2. _____

       _____

    3. _____

       _____

20_____

    1. _____

       _____

    2. _____

       _____

    3. _____

       _____

20_____

    1. _____

       _____

    2. _____

       _____

    3. _____

       _____

MARCH 12

20_____

   1. _____

     _____

   2. _____

     _____

   3. _____

     _____

20_____

   1. _____

     _____

   2. _____

     _____

   3. _____

     _____

20_____

   1. _____

     _____

   2. _____

     _____

   3. _____

     _____

MARCH 13

20_____

   1. _____

      _____

   2. _____

      _____

   3. _____

      _____

20_____

   1. _____

      _____

   2. _____

      _____

   3. _____

      _____

20_____

   1. _____

      _____

   2. _____

      _____

   3. _____

      _____

MARCH 14

20_____

1. _____
   _____

2. _____
   _____

3. _____
   _____

20_____

1. _____
   _____

2. _____
   _____

3. _____
   _____

20_____

1. _____
   _____

2. _____
   _____

3. _____
   _____

MARCH 15

20_____

1. _____
   _____
2. _____
   _____
3. _____
   _____

20_____

1. _____
   _____
2. _____
   _____
3. _____
   _____

20_____

1. _____
   _____
2. _____
   _____
3. _____
   _____

MARCH 16

20_____

1. _____

2. _____

3. _____

20_____

1. _____

2. _____

3. _____

20_____

1. _____

2. _____

3. _____

MARCH 17

20_____

  1. _____

  _____

  2. _____

  _____

  3. _____

  _____

20_____

  1. _____

  _____

  2. _____

  _____

  3. _____

  _____

20_____

  1. _____

  _____

  2. _____

  _____

  3. _____

  _____

MARCH 18

20_____

   1. _____

   _____

   2. _____

   _____

   3. _____

   _____

20_____

   1. _____

   _____

   2. _____

   _____

   3. _____

   _____

20_____

   1. _____

   _____

   2. _____

   _____

   3. _____

   _____

MARCH 19

20_____

1. _____
   _____
2. _____
   _____
3. _____
   _____

20_____

1. _____
   _____
2. _____
   _____
3. _____
   _____

20_____

1. _____
   _____
2. _____
   _____
3. _____
   _____

MARCH 20

20_____

    1. _____

    _____

    2. _____

    _____

    3. _____

    _____

20_____

    1. _____

    _____

    2. _____

    _____

    3. _____

    _____

20_____

    1. _____

    _____

    2. _____

    _____

    3. _____

    _____

MARCH 21

20_____

1. _____

_____

2. _____

_____

3. _____

_____

20_____

1. _____

_____

2. _____

_____

3. _____

_____

20_____

1. _____

_____

2. _____

_____

3. _____

_____

MARCH 22

20_____

   1. _____

     _____

   2. _____

     _____

   3. _____

     _____

20_____

   1. _____

     _____

   2. _____

     _____

   3. _____

     _____

20_____

   1. _____

     _____

   2. _____

     _____

   3. _____

     _____

MARCH 23

20_____

1. _____

_____

2. _____

_____

3. _____

_____

20_____

1. _____

_____

2. _____

_____

3. _____

_____

20_____

1. _____

_____

2. _____

_____

3. _____

_____

MARCH 24

20_____

   1. _____

   _____

   2. _____

   _____

   3. _____

   _____

20_____

   1. _____

   _____

   2. _____

   _____

   3. _____

   _____

20_____

   1. _____

   _____

   2. _____

   _____

   3. _____

   _____

MARCH 25

20_____

1. _____
   _____
2. _____
   _____
3. _____
   _____

20_____

1. _____
   _____
2. _____
   _____
3. _____
   _____

20_____

1. _____
   _____
2. _____
   _____
3. _____
   _____

MARCH 26

20_____

1. _____

_____

2. _____

_____

3. _____

_____

20_____

1. _____

_____

2. _____

_____

3. _____

_____

20_____

1. _____

_____

2. _____

_____

3. _____

_____

MARCH 27

20_____

   1. _____

    _____

   2. _____

    _____

   3. _____

    _____

20_____

   1. _____

    _____

   2. _____

    _____

   3. _____

    _____

20_____

   1. _____

    _____

   2. _____

    _____

   3. _____

    _____

MARCH 28

20_____

1. _____
   _____

2. _____
   _____

3. _____
   _____

20_____

1. _____
   _____

2. _____
   _____

3. _____
   _____

20_____

1. _____
   _____

2. _____
   _____

3. _____
   _____

MARCH 29

20_____

1. _____
   _____
2. _____
   _____
3. _____
   _____

20_____

1. _____
   _____
2. _____
   _____
3. _____
   _____

20_____

1. _____
   _____
2. _____
   _____
3. _____
   _____

MARCH 30

20_____

1. _____
   _____

2. _____
   _____

3. _____
   _____

20_____

1. _____
   _____

2. _____
   _____

3. _____
   _____

20_____

1. _____
   _____

2. _____
   _____

3. _____
   _____

MARCH 31

20_____

1. _____
   _____

2. _____
   _____

3. _____
   _____

20_____

1. _____
   _____

2. _____
   _____

3. _____
   _____

20_____

1. _____
   _____

2. _____
   _____

3. _____
   _____

APRIL 1

0 _____

  1. _____

  _____

  2. _____

  _____

  3. _____

  _____

0 _____

  1. _____

  _____

  2. _____

  _____

  3. _____

  _____

0 _____

  1. _____

  _____

  2. _____

  _____

  3. _____

  _____

APRIL 2

20_____

   1. _____

     _____

   2. _____

     _____

   3. _____

     _____

20_____

   1. _____

     _____

   2. _____

     _____

   3. _____

     _____

20_____

   1. _____

     _____

   2. _____

     _____

   3. _____

     _____

APRIL 3

○ _____

1. _____
   _____
2. _____
   _____
3. _____
   _____

○ _____

1. _____
   _____
2. _____
   _____
3. _____
   _____

○ _____

1. _____
   _____
2. _____
   _____
3. _____
   _____

APRIL 4

20_____

1. _____

_____

2. _____

_____

3. _____

_____

20_____

1. _____

_____

2. _____

_____

3. _____

_____

20_____

1. _____

_____

2. _____

_____

3. _____

_____

APRIL 5

◯ _____

1. _____

   _____

2. _____

   _____

3. _____

   _____

◯ _____

1. _____

   _____

2. _____

   _____

3. _____

   _____

◯ _____

1. _____

   _____

2. _____

   _____

3. _____

   _____

APRIL 6

20_____

  1. _____

  _____

  2. _____

  _____

  3. _____

  _____

20_____

  1. _____

  _____

  2. _____

  _____

  3. _____

  _____

20_____

  1. _____

  _____

  2. _____

  _____

  3. _____

  _____

APRIL 7

)_____

1. _____
   _____
2. _____
   _____
3. _____
   _____

)_____

1. _____
   _____
2. _____
   _____
3. _____
   _____

)_____

1. _____
   _____
2. _____
   _____
3. _____
   _____

APRIL 8

20_____

1. _____
   _____
2. _____
   _____
3. _____
   _____

20_____

1. _____
   _____
2. _____
   _____
3. _____
   _____

20_____

1. _____
   _____
2. _____
   _____
3. _____
   _____

APRIL 9

O_____

1. _____
_____

2. _____
_____

3. _____
_____

O_____

1. _____
_____

2. _____
_____

3. _____
_____

O_____

1. _____
_____

2. _____
_____

3. _____
_____

APRIL 10

20_____

1. _____
   _____
2. _____
   _____
3. _____
   _____

20_____

1. _____
   _____
2. _____
   _____
3. _____
   _____

20_____

1. _____
   _____
2. _____
   _____
3. _____
   _____

APRIL 11

0 _____

1. _____
   _____

2. _____
   _____

3. _____
   _____

0 _____

1. _____
   _____

2. _____
   _____

3. _____
   _____

0 _____

1. _____
   _____

2. _____
   _____

3. _____
   _____

APRIL 12

20_____

   1. _____

      _____

   2. _____

      _____

   3. _____

      _____

20_____

   1. _____

      _____

   2. _____

      _____

   3. _____

      _____

20_____

   1. _____

      _____

   2. _____

      _____

   3. _____

      _____

APRIL 13

0 _____

   1. _____

   _____

   2. _____

   _____

   3. _____

   _____

0 _____

   1. _____

   _____

   2. _____

   _____

   3. _____

   _____

20 _____

   1. _____

   _____

   2. _____

   _____

   3. _____

   _____

APRIL 14

20_____

1. _____
_____
2. _____
_____
3. _____
_____

20_____

1. _____
_____
2. _____
_____
3. _____
_____

20_____

1. _____
_____
2. _____
_____
3. _____
_____

APRIL 15

20_____

   1. _____

      _____

   2. _____

      _____

   3. _____

      _____

20_____

   1. _____

      _____

   2. _____

      _____

   3. _____

      _____

20_____

   1. _____

      _____

   2. _____

      _____

   3. _____

      _____

APRIL 16

20_____

1. _____
   _____
2. _____
   _____
3. _____
   _____

20_____

1. _____
   _____
2. _____
   _____
3. _____
   _____

20_____

1. _____
   _____
2. _____
   _____
3. _____
   _____

APRIL 17

20 _____

1. _____

_____

2. _____

_____

3. _____

_____

20 _____

1. _____

_____

2. _____

_____

3. _____

_____

20 _____

1. _____

_____

2. _____

_____

3. _____

_____

APRIL 18

20_____

   1. _____

      _____

   2. _____

      _____

   3. _____

      _____

20_____

   1. _____

      _____

   2. _____

      _____

   3. _____

      _____

20_____

   1. _____

      _____

   2. _____

      _____

   3. _____

      _____

APRIL 19

20_____

1. _____

_____

2. _____

_____

3. _____

_____

20_____

1. _____

_____

2. _____

_____

3. _____

_____

20_____

1. _____

_____

2. _____

_____

3. _____

_____

APRIL 20

20_____

1. _____
   _____

2. _____
   _____

3. _____
   _____

20_____

1. _____
   _____

2. _____
   _____

3. _____
   _____

20_____

1. _____
   _____

2. _____
   _____

3. _____
   _____

APRIL 21

20_____

    1. _____

       _____

    2. _____

       _____

    3. _____

       _____

20_____

    1. _____

       _____

    2. _____

       _____

    3. _____

       _____

20_____

    1. _____

       _____

    2. _____

       _____

    3. _____

       _____

APRIL 22

20_____

1. _____

   _____

2. _____

   _____

3. _____

   _____

20_____

1. _____

   _____

2. _____

   _____

3. _____

   _____

20_____

1. _____

   _____

2. _____

   _____

3. _____

   _____

APRIL 23

20_____

1. _____
   _____
2. _____
   _____
3. _____
   _____

20_____

1. _____
   _____
2. _____
   _____
3. _____
   _____

20_____

1. _____
   _____
2. _____
   _____
3. _____
   _____

APRIL 24

20_____

1. _____

_____

2. _____

_____

3. _____

_____

20_____

1. _____

_____

2. _____

_____

3. _____

_____

20_____

1. _____

_____

2. _____

_____

3. _____

_____

APRIL 25

0 _____

1. _____
   _____

2. _____
   _____

3. _____
   _____

0 _____

1. _____
   _____

2. _____
   _____

3. _____
   _____

0 _____

1. _____
   _____

2. _____
   _____

3. _____
   _____

APRIL 26

20_____

1. _____
   _____
2. _____
   _____
3. _____
   _____

20_____

1. _____
   _____
2. _____
   _____
3. _____
   _____

20_____

1. _____
   _____
2. _____
   _____
3. _____
   _____

APRIL 27

○ _____

1. _____
   _____

2. _____
   _____

3. _____
   _____

○ _____

1. _____
   _____

2. _____
   _____

3. _____
   _____

○ _____

1. _____
   _____

2. _____
   _____

3. _____
   _____

APRIL 28

20_____

   1. _____

     _____

   2. _____

     _____

   3. _____

     _____

20_____

   1. _____

     _____

   2. _____

     _____

   3. _____

     _____

20_____

   1. _____

     _____

   2. _____

     _____

   3. _____

     _____

APRIL 29

)_____

1. _____
   _____
2. _____
   _____
3. _____
   _____

)_____

1. _____
   _____
2. _____
   _____
3. _____
   _____

)_____

1. _____
   _____
2. _____
   _____
3. _____
   _____

APRIL 30

20_____

   1. _____
      _____

   2. _____
      _____

   3. _____
      _____

20_____

   1. _____
      _____

   2. _____
      _____

   3. _____
      _____

20_____

   1. _____
      _____

   2. _____
      _____

   3. _____
      _____

MAY 1

〇 _____

1. _____
   _____
2. _____
   _____
3. _____
   _____

〇 _____

1. _____
   _____
2. _____
   _____
3. _____
   _____

〇 _____

1. _____
   _____
2. _____
   _____
3. _____
   _____

MAY 2

20_____

1. _____
   _____
2. _____
   _____
3. _____
   _____

20_____

1. _____
   _____
2. _____
   _____
3. _____
   _____

20_____

1. _____
   _____
2. _____
   _____
3. _____
   _____

MAY 3

O_____

1. _____

2. _____

3. _____

O_____

1. _____

2. _____

3. _____

O_____

1. _____

2. _____

3. _____

MAY 4

20_____

1. _____
_____

2. _____
_____

3. _____
_____

20_____

1. _____
_____

2. _____
_____

3. _____
_____

20_____

1. _____
_____

2. _____
_____

3. _____
_____

MAY 5

)_____

1. _____
   _____
2. _____
   _____
3. _____
   _____

)_____

1. _____
   _____
2. _____
   _____
3. _____
   _____

)_____

1. _____
   _____
2. _____
   _____
3. _____
   _____

MAY 6

20_____

   1. _____
_____

   2. _____
_____

   3. _____
_____

20_____

   1. _____
_____

   2. _____
_____

   3. _____
_____

20_____

   1. _____
_____

   2. _____
_____

   3. _____
_____

MAY 7

) _____

1. _____

_____

2. _____

_____

3. _____

_____

) _____

1. _____

_____

2. _____

_____

3. _____

_____

) _____

1. _____

_____

2. _____

_____

3. _____

_____

MAY 8

20_____

1. _____
   _____

2. _____
   _____

3. _____
   _____

20_____

1. _____
   _____

2. _____
   _____

3. _____
   _____

20_____

1. _____
   _____

2. _____
   _____

3. _____
   _____

MAY 9

_____

1. _____

_____

2. _____

_____

3. _____

_____

_____

1. _____

_____

2. _____

_____

3. _____

_____

_____

1. _____

_____

2. _____

_____

3. _____

_____

MAY 10

20_____

1. _____

2. _____

3. _____

20_____

1. _____

2. _____

3. _____

20_____

1. _____

2. _____

3. _____

MAY 11

) _____

1. _____
   _____
2. _____
   _____
3. _____
   _____

) _____

1. _____
   _____
2. _____
   _____
3. _____
   _____

) _____

1. _____
   _____
2. _____
   _____
3. _____
   _____

MAY 12

20____

   1. _____

   _____

   2. _____

   _____

   3. _____

   _____

20____

   1. _____

   _____

   2. _____

   _____

   3. _____

   _____

20____

   1. _____

   _____

   2. _____

   _____

   3. _____

   _____

MAY 13

) _____

1. _____
   _____

2. _____
   _____

3. _____
   _____

) _____

1. _____
   _____

2. _____
   _____

3. _____
   _____

) _____

1. _____
   _____

2. _____
   _____

3. _____
   _____

MAY 14

20_____

1. _____
   _____
2. _____
   _____
3. _____
   _____

20_____

1. _____
   _____
2. _____
   _____
3. _____
   _____

20_____

1. _____
   _____
2. _____
   _____
3. _____
   _____

MAY 15

20_____

1. _____
   _____
2. _____
   _____
3. _____
   _____

20_____

1. _____
   _____
2. _____
   _____
3. _____
   _____

20_____

1. _____
   _____
2. _____
   _____
3. _____
   _____

MAY 16

20_____

1. _____

   _____

2. _____

   _____

3. _____

   _____

20_____

1. _____

   _____

2. _____

   _____

3. _____

   _____

20_____

1. _____

   _____

2. _____

   _____

3. _____

   _____

MAY 17

O_____

1. _____

_____

2. _____

_____

3. _____

_____

O_____

1. _____

_____

2. _____

_____

3. _____

_____

O_____

1. _____

_____

2. _____

_____

3. _____

_____

MAY 18

20_____

   1. _____

     _____

   2. _____

     _____

   3. _____

     _____

20_____

   1. _____

     _____

   2. _____

     _____

   3. _____

     _____

20_____

   1. _____

     _____

   2. _____

     _____

   3. _____

     _____

MAY 19

20_____

   1. _____

   _____

   2. _____

   _____

   3. _____

   _____

20_____

   1. _____

   _____

   2. _____

   _____

   3. _____

   _____

20_____

   1. _____

   _____

   2. _____

   _____

   3. _____

   _____

MAY 20

20_____

   1. _____

     _____

   2. _____

     _____

   3. _____

     _____

20_____

   1. _____

     _____

   2. _____

     _____

   3. _____

     _____

20_____

   1. _____

     _____

   2. _____

     _____

   3. _____

     _____

MAY 21

0_____

1. _____

   _____

2. _____

   _____

3. _____

   _____

0_____

1. _____

   _____

2. _____

   _____

3. _____

   _____

0_____

1. _____

   _____

2. _____

   _____

3. _____

   _____

MAY 22

20_____

    1. _____

    _____

    2. _____

    _____

    3. _____

    _____

20_____

    1. _____

    _____

    2. _____

    _____

    3. _____

    _____

20_____

    1. _____

    _____

    2. _____

    _____

    3. _____

    _____

MAY 23

20_____

1. _____

   _____

2. _____

   _____

3. _____

   _____

20_____

1. _____

   _____

2. _____

   _____

3. _____

   _____

20_____

1. _____

   _____

2. _____

   _____

3. _____

   _____

MAY 24

20_____

   1. _____

   _____

   2. _____

   _____

   3. _____

   _____

20_____

   1. _____

   _____

   2. _____

   _____

   3. _____

   _____

20_____

   1. _____

   _____

   2. _____

   _____

   3. _____

   _____

MAY 25

20_____

1. _____
   _____
2. _____
   _____
3. _____
   _____

20_____

1. _____
   _____
2. _____
   _____
3. _____
   _____

20_____

1. _____
   _____
2. _____
   _____
3. _____
   _____

MAY 26

20_____

1. _____
   _____
2. _____
   _____
3. _____
   _____

20_____

1. _____
   _____
2. _____
   _____
3. _____
   _____

20_____

1. _____
   _____
2. _____
   _____
3. _____
   _____

MAY 27

0_____

1. _____
   _____
2. _____
   _____
3. _____
   _____

0_____

1. _____
   _____
2. _____
   _____
3. _____
   _____

0_____

1. _____
   _____
2. _____
   _____
3. _____
   _____

MAY 28

20_____

1. _____

_____

2. _____

_____

3. _____

_____

20_____

1. _____

_____

2. _____

_____

3. _____

_____

20_____

1. _____

_____

2. _____

_____

3. _____

_____

MAY 29

0 _____

   1. _____

     _____

   2. _____

     _____

   3. _____

     _____

0 _____

   1. _____

     _____

   2. _____

     _____

   3. _____

     _____

0 _____

   1. _____

     _____

   2. _____

     _____

   3. _____

     _____

20_____

   1. _____
   _____

   2. _____
   _____

   3. _____
   _____

20_____

   1. _____
   _____

   2. _____
   _____

   3. _____
   _____

20_____

   1. _____
   _____

   2. _____
   _____

   3. _____
   _____

MAY 31

O_____

1. _____

_____

2. _____

_____

3. _____

_____

O_____

1. _____

_____

2. _____

_____

3. _____

_____

O_____

1. _____

_____

2. _____

_____

3. _____

_____

JUNE 1

20_____

1. _____
   _____

2. _____
   _____

3. _____
   _____

20_____

1. _____
   _____

2. _____
   _____

3. _____
   _____

20_____

1. _____
   _____

2. _____
   _____

3. _____
   _____

JUNE 2

0_____

1. _____

_____

2. _____

_____

3. _____

_____

0_____

1. _____

_____

2. _____

_____

3. _____

_____

0_____

1. _____

_____

2. _____

_____

3. _____

_____

JUNE 3

20_____

1. _____
   _____
2. _____
   _____
3. _____
   _____

20_____

1. _____
   _____
2. _____
   _____
3. _____
   _____

20_____

1. _____
   _____
2. _____
   _____
3. _____
   _____

JUNE 4

○ _____

1. _____
   _____

2. _____
   _____

3. _____
   _____

○ _____

1. _____
   _____

2. _____
   _____

3. _____
   _____

○ _____

1. _____
   _____

2. _____
   _____

3. _____
   _____

JUNE 5

20_____

1. _____
   _____
2. _____
   _____
3. _____
   _____

20_____

1. _____
   _____
2. _____
   _____
3. _____
   _____

20_____

1. _____
   _____
2. _____
   _____
3. _____
   _____

JUNE 6

) _____

1. _____
   _____

2. _____
   _____

3. _____
   _____

) _____

1. _____
   _____

2. _____
   _____

3. _____
   _____

) _____

1. _____
   _____

2. _____
   _____

3. _____
   _____

JUNE 7

20_____

1. _____
_____

2. _____
_____

3. _____
_____

20_____

1. _____
_____

2. _____
_____

3. _____
_____

20_____

1. _____
_____

2. _____
_____

3. _____
_____

JUNE 8

20_____

1. _____
   _____
2. _____
   _____
3. _____
   _____

20_____

1. _____
   _____
2. _____
   _____
3. _____
   _____

20_____

1. _____
   _____
2. _____
   _____
3. _____
   _____

JUNE 9

20_____

1. _____

_____

2. _____

_____

3. _____

_____

20_____

1. _____

_____

2. _____

_____

3. _____

_____

20_____

1. _____

_____

2. _____

_____

3. _____

_____

JUNE 10

20 _____

1. _____
   _____
2. _____
   _____
3. _____
   _____

20 _____

1. _____
   _____
2. _____
   _____
3. _____
   _____

20 _____

1. _____
   _____
2. _____
   _____
3. _____
   _____

JUNE 11

20_____

    1. _____

    _____

    2. _____

    _____

    3. _____

    _____

20_____

    1. _____

    _____

    2. _____

    _____

    3. _____

    _____

20_____

    1. _____

    _____

    2. _____

    _____

    3. _____

    _____

JUNE 12

_____

1. _____

_____

2. _____

_____

3. _____

_____

_____

1. _____

_____

2. _____

_____

3. _____

_____

_____

1. _____

_____

2. _____

_____

3. _____

_____

JUNE 13

20_____

   1. _____

     _____

   2. _____

     _____

   3. _____

     _____

20_____

   1. _____

     _____

   2. _____

     _____

   3. _____

     _____

20_____

   1. _____

     _____

   2. _____

     _____

   3. _____

     _____

JUNE 14

◗ _____

1. _____
   _____

2. _____
   _____

3. _____
   _____

◗ _____

1. _____
   _____

2. _____
   _____

3. _____
   _____

◗ _____

1. _____
   _____

2. _____
   _____

3. _____
   _____

JUNE 15

20_____

   1. _____

   _____

   2. _____

   _____

   3. _____

   _____

20_____

   1. _____

   _____

   2. _____

   _____

   3. _____

   _____

20_____

   1. _____

   _____

   2. _____

   _____

   3. _____

   _____

JUNE 16

◯ _____

   1. _____

   _____

   2. _____

   _____

   3. _____

   _____

◯ _____

   1. _____

   _____

   2. _____

   _____

   3. _____

   _____

◯ _____

   1. _____

   _____

   2. _____

   _____

   3. _____

   _____

JUNE 17

20_____

1. _____
   _____

2. _____
   _____

3. _____
   _____

20_____

1. _____
   _____

2. _____
   _____

3. _____
   _____

20_____

1. _____
   _____

2. _____
   _____

3. _____
   _____

JUNE 18

20 _____

1. _____
   _____
2. _____
   _____
3. _____
   _____

20 _____

1. _____
   _____
2. _____
   _____
3. _____
   _____

20 _____

1. _____
   _____
2. _____
   _____
3. _____
   _____

JUNE 19

20_____

1. _____

_____

2. _____

_____

3. _____

_____

20_____

1. _____

_____

2. _____

_____

3. _____

_____

20_____

1. _____

_____

2. _____

_____

3. _____

_____

JUNE 20

20_____

1. _____
   _____

2. _____
   _____

3. _____
   _____

20_____

1. _____
   _____

2. _____
   _____

3. _____
   _____

20_____

1. _____
   _____

2. _____
   _____

3. _____
   _____

JUNE 21

20_____

1. _____

_____

2. _____

_____

3. _____

_____

20_____

1. _____

_____

2. _____

_____

3. _____

_____

20_____

1. _____

_____

2. _____

_____

3. _____

_____

JUNE 22

20_____

1. _____
   _____
2. _____
   _____
3. _____
   _____

20_____

1. _____
   _____
2. _____
   _____
3. _____
   _____

20_____

1. _____
   _____
2. _____
   _____
3. _____
   _____

JUNE 23

20_____

1. _____
   _____
2. _____
   _____
3. _____
   _____

20_____

1. _____
   _____
2. _____
   _____
3. _____
   _____

20_____

1. _____
   _____
2. _____
   _____
3. _____
   _____

JUNE 24

0 _____

1. _____
   _____

2. _____
   _____

3. _____
   _____

0 _____

1. _____
   _____

2. _____
   _____

3. _____
   _____

0 _____

1. _____
   _____

2. _____
   _____

3. _____
   _____

JUNE 25

20_____

   1. _____

      _____

   2. _____

      _____

   3. _____

      _____

20_____

   1. _____

      _____

   2. _____

      _____

   3. _____

      _____

20_____

   1. _____

      _____

   2. _____

      _____

   3. _____

      _____

JUNE 26

0_____

1. _____

_____

2. _____

_____

3. _____

_____

0_____

1. _____

_____

2. _____

_____

3. _____

_____

0_____

1. _____

_____

2. _____

_____

3. _____

_____

JUNE 27

20_____

1. _____
_____

2. _____
_____

3. _____
_____

20_____

1. _____
_____

2. _____
_____

3. _____
_____

20_____

1. _____
_____

2. _____
_____

3. _____
_____

JUNE 28

0 _____

1. _____

_____

2. _____

_____

3. _____

_____

0 _____

1. _____

_____

2. _____

_____

3. _____

_____

0 _____

1. _____

_____

2. _____

_____

3. _____

_____

JUNE 29

20_____

1. _____

_____

2. _____

_____

3. _____

_____

20_____

1. _____

_____

2. _____

_____

3. _____

_____

20_____

1. _____

_____

2. _____

_____

3. _____

_____

JUNE 30

20_____

1. _____

_____

2. _____

_____

3. _____

_____

20_____

1. _____

_____

2. _____

_____

3. _____

_____

20_____

1. _____

_____

2. _____

_____

3. _____

_____

JULY 1

20_____

    1. _____

    _____

    2. _____

    _____

    3. _____

    _____

20_____

    1. _____

    _____

    2. _____

    _____

    3. _____

    _____

20_____

    1. _____

    _____

    2. _____

    _____

    3. _____

    _____

JULY 2

0_____

1. _____
_____

2. _____
_____

3. _____
_____

0_____

1. _____
_____

2. _____
_____

3. _____
_____

0_____

1. _____
_____

2. _____
_____

3. _____
_____

JULY 3

20_____

   1. _____

     _____

   2. _____

     _____

   3. _____

     _____

20_____

   1. _____

     _____

   2. _____

     _____

   3. _____

     _____

20_____

   1. _____

     _____

   2. _____

     _____

   3. _____

     _____

JULY 4

0 _____

  1. _____

    _____

  2. _____

    _____

  3. _____

    _____

0 _____

  1. _____

    _____

  2. _____

    _____

  3. _____

    _____

0 _____

  1. _____

    _____

  2. _____

    _____

  3. _____

    _____

JULY 5

20_____

    1. _____

    _____

    2. _____

    _____

    3. _____

    _____

20_____

    1. _____

    _____

    2. _____

    _____

    3. _____

    _____

20_____

    1. _____

    _____

    2. _____

    _____

    3. _____

    _____

JULY 6

) _____

1. _____
   _____
2. _____
   _____
3. _____
   _____

) _____

1. _____
   _____
2. _____
   _____
3. _____
   _____

) _____

1. _____
   _____
2. _____
   _____
3. _____
   _____

JULY 7

20_____

   1. _____

     _____

   2. _____

     _____

   3. _____

     _____

20_____

   1. _____

     _____

   2. _____

     _____

   3. _____

     _____

20_____

   1. _____

     _____

   2. _____

     _____

   3. _____

     _____

JULY 8

_____

1. _____

_____

2. _____

_____

3. _____

_____

_____

1. _____

_____

2. _____

_____

3. _____

_____

_____

1. _____

_____

2. _____

_____

3. _____

_____

JULY 9

20_____

   1. _____

   _____

   2. _____

   _____

   3. _____

   _____

20_____

   1. _____

   _____

   2. _____

   _____

   3. _____

   _____

20_____

   1. _____

   _____

   2. _____

   _____

   3. _____

   _____

JULY 10

)_____

1. _____

_____

2. _____

_____

3. _____

_____

)_____

1. _____

_____

2. _____

_____

3. _____

_____

)_____

1. _____

_____

2. _____

_____

3. _____

_____

JULY 11

20_____

1. _____
   _____

2. _____
   _____

3. _____
   _____

20_____

1. _____
   _____

2. _____
   _____

3. _____
   _____

20_____

1. _____
   _____

2. _____
   _____

3. _____
   _____

JULY 12

20_____

1. _____
   _____

2. _____
   _____

3. _____
   _____

20_____

1. _____
   _____

2. _____
   _____

3. _____
   _____

20_____

1. _____
   _____

2. _____
   _____

3. _____
   _____

JULY 13

20_____

   1. _____
     _____

   2. _____
     _____

   3. _____
     _____

20_____

   1. _____
     _____

   2. _____
     _____

   3. _____
     _____

20_____

   1. _____
     _____

   2. _____
     _____

   3. _____
     _____

JULY 14

20_____

1. _____

_____

2. _____

_____

3. _____

_____

20_____

1. _____

_____

2. _____

_____

3. _____

_____

20_____

1. _____

_____

2. _____

_____

3. _____

_____

JULY 15

20_____

    1. _____

    _____

    2. _____

    _____

    3. _____

    _____

20_____

    1. _____

    _____

    2. _____

    _____

    3. _____

    _____

20_____

    1. _____

    _____

    2. _____

    _____

    3. _____

    _____

JULY 16

)_____

1. _____

2. _____

3. _____

)_____

1. _____

2. _____

3. _____

)_____

1. _____

2. _____

3. _____

JULY 17

20_____

   1. _____

   _____

   2. _____

   _____

   3. _____

   _____

20_____

   1. _____

   _____

   2. _____

   _____

   3. _____

   _____

20_____

   1. _____

   _____

   2. _____

   _____

   3. _____

   _____

JULY 18

0 _____

  1. _____
_____

  2. _____
_____

  3. _____
_____

0 _____

  1. _____
_____

  2. _____
_____

  3. _____
_____

0 _____

  1. _____
_____

  2. _____
_____

  3. _____
_____

JULY 19

20_____

1. _____
   _____
2. _____
   _____
3. _____
   _____

20_____

1. _____
   _____
2. _____
   _____
3. _____
   _____

20_____

1. _____
   _____
2. _____
   _____
3. _____
   _____

JULY 20

20 _____

   1. _____

     _____

   2. _____

     _____

   3. _____

     _____

20 _____

   1. _____

     _____

   2. _____

     _____

   3. _____

     _____

20 _____

   1. _____

     _____

   2. _____

     _____

   3. _____

     _____

JULY 21

20_____

　1. _____

　　 _____

　2. _____

　　 _____

　3. _____

　　 _____

20_____

　1. _____

　　 _____

　　 _____

　　 _____

　3. _____

　　 _____

20_____

　1. _____

　　 _____

　2. _____

　　 _____

　3. _____

　　 _____

JULY 22

20_____

   1. _____

     _____

   2. _____

     _____

   3. _____

     _____

20_____

   1. _____

     _____

   2. _____

     _____

   3. _____

     _____

20_____

   1. _____

     _____

   2. _____

     _____

   3. _____

     _____

JULY 23

20_____

   1. _____
     _____
   2. _____
     _____
   3. _____
     _____

20_____

   1. _____
     _____
   2. _____
     _____
   3. _____
     _____

20_____

   1. _____
     _____
   2. _____
     _____
   3. _____
     _____

JULY 24

20_____

1. _____

_____

2. _____

_____

3. _____

_____

20_____

1. _____

_____

2. _____

_____

3. _____

_____

20_____

1. _____

_____

2. _____

_____

3. _____

_____

JULY 25

20_____

   1. _____

     _____

   2. _____

     _____

   3. _____

     _____

20_____

   1. _____

     _____

   2. _____

     _____

   3. _____

     _____

20_____

   1. _____

     _____

   2. _____

     _____

   3. _____

     _____

JULY 26

20_____

1. _____
   _____

2. _____
   _____

3. _____
   _____

20_____

1. _____
   _____

2. _____
   _____

3. _____
   _____

20_____

1. _____
   _____

2. _____
   _____

3. _____
   _____

JULY 27

20_____

   1. _____

   _____

   2. _____

   _____

   3. _____

   _____

20_____

   1. _____

   _____

   2. _____

   _____

   3. _____

   _____

20_____

   1. _____

   _____

   2. _____

   _____

   3. _____

   _____

JULY 28

20_____

1. _____
   _____

2. _____
   _____

3. _____
   _____

20_____

1. _____
   _____

2. _____
   _____

3. _____
   _____

20_____

1. _____
   _____

2. _____
   _____

3. _____
   _____

JULY 29

20_____

   1. _____

   _____

   2. _____

   _____

   3. _____

   _____

20_____

   1. _____

   _____

   2. _____

   _____

   3. _____

   _____

20_____

   1. _____

   _____

   2. _____

   _____

   3. _____

   _____

JULY 30

20_____

1. _____
_____

2. _____
_____

3. _____
_____

20_____

1. _____
_____

2. _____
_____

3. _____
_____

20_____

1. _____
_____

2. _____
_____

3. _____
_____

JULY 31

20_____

   1. _____

     _____

   2. _____

     _____

   3. _____

     _____

20_____

   1. _____

     _____

   2. _____

     _____

   3. _____

     _____

20_____

   1. _____

     _____

   2. _____

     _____

   3. _____

     _____

AUGUST 1

20_____

1. _____

_____

2. _____

_____

3. _____

_____

20_____

1. _____

_____

2. _____

_____

3. _____

_____

20_____

1. _____

_____

2. _____

_____

3. _____

_____

AUGUST 2

20_____

   1. _____

     _____

   2. _____

     _____

   3. _____

     _____

20_____

   1. _____

     _____

   2. _____

     _____

   3. _____

     _____

20_____

   1. _____

     _____

   2. _____

     _____

   3. _____

     _____

AUGUST 3

20_____

1. _____

_____

2. _____

_____

3. _____

_____

20_____

1. _____

_____

2. _____

_____

3. _____

_____

20_____

1. _____

_____

2. _____

_____

3. _____

_____

AUGUST 4

20_____

1. _____
   _____
2. _____
   _____
3. _____
   _____

20_____

1. _____
   _____
2. _____
   _____
3. _____
   _____

20_____

1. _____
   _____
2. _____
   _____
3. _____
   _____

AUGUST 5

20_____

1. _____
   _____
2. _____
   _____
3. _____
   _____

20_____

1. _____
   _____
2. _____
   _____
3. _____
   _____

20_____

1. _____
   _____
2. _____
   _____
3. _____
   _____

AUGUST 6

20_____

   1. _____
      _____

   2. _____
      _____

   3. _____
      _____

20_____

   1. _____
      _____

   2. _____
      _____

   3. _____
      _____

20_____

   1. _____
      _____

   2. _____
      _____

   3. _____
      _____

AUGUST 7

O _____

1. _____
   _____
2. _____
   _____
3. _____
   _____

O _____

1. _____
   _____
2. _____
   _____
3. _____
   _____

O _____

1. _____
   _____
2. _____
   _____
3. _____
   _____

AUGUST 8

20_____

1. _____
   _____

2. _____
   _____

3. _____
   _____

20_____

1. _____
   _____

2. _____
   _____

3. _____
   _____

20_____

1. _____
   _____

2. _____
   _____

3. _____
   _____

AUGUST 9

◯ _____

1. _____
   _____
2. _____
   _____
3. _____
   _____

◯ _____

1. _____
   _____
2. _____
   _____
3. _____
   _____

◯ _____

1. _____
   _____
2. _____
   _____
3. _____
   _____

AUGUST 10

20_____

    1. _____

    _____

    2. _____

    _____

    3. _____

    _____

20_____

    1. _____

    _____

    2. _____

    _____

    3. _____

    _____

20_____

    1. _____

    _____

    2. _____

    _____

    3. _____

    _____

AUGUST 11

0 _____

1. _____
   _____
2. _____
   _____
3. _____
   _____

0 _____

1. _____
   _____
2. _____
   _____
3. _____
   _____

0 _____

1. _____
   _____
2. _____
   _____
3. _____
   _____

AUGUST 12

20_____

1. _____

_____

2. _____

_____

3. _____

_____

20_____

1. _____

_____

2. _____

_____

3. _____

_____

20_____

1. _____

_____

2. _____

_____

3. _____

_____

AUGUST 13

O _____

1. _____
   _____

2. _____
   _____

3. _____
   _____

O _____

1. _____
   _____

2. _____
   _____

3. _____
   _____

O _____

1. _____
   _____

2. _____
   _____

3. _____
   _____

AUGUST 14

20_____

1. _____
   _____
2. _____
   _____
3. _____
   _____

20_____

1. _____
   _____
2. _____
   _____
3. _____
   _____

20_____

1. _____
   _____
2. _____
   _____
3. _____
   _____

AUGUST 15

_____

1. _____
   _____
2. _____
   _____
3. _____
   _____

_____

1. _____
   _____
2. _____
   _____
3. _____
   _____

_____

1. _____
   _____
2. _____
   _____
3. _____
   _____

AUGUST 16

20_____

1. _____
_____

2. _____
_____

3. _____
_____

20_____

1. _____
_____

2. _____
_____

3. _____
_____

20_____

1. _____
_____

2. _____
_____

3. _____
_____

AUGUST 17

)_____

1. _____

_____

2. _____

_____

3. _____

_____

)_____

1. _____

_____

2. _____

_____

3. _____

_____

)_____

1. _____

_____

2. _____

_____

3. _____

_____

AUGUST 18

20_____

   1. _____

     _____

   2. _____

     _____

   3. _____

     _____

20_____

   1. _____

     _____

   2. _____

     _____

   3. _____

     _____

20_____

   1. _____

     _____

   2. _____

     _____

   3. _____

     _____

AUGUST 19

)_____

1. _____
   _____
2. _____
   _____
3. _____
   _____

)_____

1. _____
   _____
2. _____
   _____
3. _____
   _____

0_____

1. _____
   _____
2. _____
   _____
3. _____
   _____

AUGUST 20

20_____

1. _____
   _____

2. _____
   _____

3. _____
   _____

20_____

1. _____
   _____

2. _____
   _____

3. _____
   _____

20_____

1. _____
   _____

2. _____
   _____

3. _____
   _____

AUGUST 21

○ _____

1. _____
   _____
2. _____
   _____
3. _____
   _____

○ _____

1. _____
   _____
2. _____
   _____
3. _____
   _____

○ _____

1. _____
   _____
2. _____
   _____
3. _____
   _____

AUGUST 22

20_____

    1. _____

    _____

    2. _____

    _____

    3. _____

    _____

20_____

    1. _____

    _____

    2. _____

    _____

    3. _____

    _____

20_____

    1. _____

    _____

    2. _____

    _____

    3. _____

    _____

AUGUST 23

20_____

1. _____
   _____

2. _____
   _____

3. _____
   _____

20_____

1. _____
   _____

2. _____
   _____

3. _____
   _____

20_____

1. _____
   _____

2. _____
   _____

3. _____
   _____

AUGUST 24

20_____

1. _____
_____

2. _____
_____

3. _____
_____

20_____

1. _____
_____

2. _____
_____

3. _____
_____

20_____

1. _____
_____

2. _____
_____

3. _____
_____

AUGUST 25

20_____

1. _____

   _____

2. _____

   _____

3. _____

   _____

20_____

1. _____

   _____

2. _____

   _____

3. _____

   _____

20_____

1. _____

   _____

2. _____

   _____

3. _____

   _____

AUGUST 26

20_____

1. _____
   _____
2. _____
   _____
3. _____
   _____

20_____

1. _____
   _____
2. _____
   _____
3. _____
   _____

20_____

1. _____
   _____
2. _____
   _____
3. _____
   _____

AUGUST 27

20_____

1. _____

   _____

2. _____

   _____

3. _____

   _____

20_____

1. _____

   _____

2. _____

   _____

3. _____

   _____

20_____

1. _____

   _____

2. _____

   _____

3. _____

   _____

AUGUST 28

20_____

1. _____

_____

2. _____

_____

3. _____

_____

20_____

1. _____

_____

2. _____

_____

3. _____

_____

20_____

1. _____

_____

2. _____

_____

3. _____

_____

AUGUST 29

0_____

1. _____

   _____

2. _____

   _____

3. _____

   _____

0_____

1. _____

   _____

2. _____

   _____

3. _____

   _____

20_____

1. _____

   _____

2. _____

   _____

3. _____

   _____

AUGUST 30

20_____

1. _____

_____

2. _____

_____

3. _____

_____

20_____

1. _____

_____

2. _____

_____

3. _____

_____

20_____

1. _____

_____

2. _____

_____

3. _____

_____

AUGUST 31

20_____

1. _____
_____

2. _____
_____

3. _____
_____

20_____

1. _____
_____

2. _____
_____

3. _____
_____

20_____

1. _____
_____

2. _____
_____

3. _____
_____

SEPTEMBER 1

20_____

   1. _____

   _____

   2. _____

   _____

   3. _____

   _____

20_____

   1. _____

   _____

   2. _____

   _____

   3. _____

   _____

20_____

   1. _____

   _____

   2. _____

   _____

   3. _____

   _____

SEPTEMBER 2

20_____

1. _____
   _____
2. _____
   _____
3. _____
   _____

20_____

1. _____
   _____
2. _____
   _____
3. _____
   _____

20_____

1. _____
   _____
2. _____
   _____
3. _____
   _____

SEPTEMBER 3

20_____

1. _____
   _____

2. _____
   _____

3. _____
   _____

20_____

1. _____
   _____

2. _____
   _____

3. _____
   _____

20_____

1. _____
   _____

2. _____
   _____

3. _____
   _____

SEPTEMBER 4

20_____

1. _____

_____

2. _____

_____

3. _____

_____

20_____

1. _____

_____

2. _____

_____

3. _____

_____

20_____

1. _____

_____

2. _____

_____

3. _____

_____

SEPTEMBER 5

20_____

1. _____
_____

2. _____
_____

3. _____
_____

20_____

1. _____
_____

2. _____
_____

3. _____
_____

20_____

1. _____
_____

2. _____
_____

3. _____
_____

SEPTEMBER 6

20_____

1. _____

_____

2. _____

_____

3. _____

_____

20_____

1. _____

_____

2. _____

_____

3. _____

_____

20_____

1. _____

_____

2. _____

_____

3. _____

_____

SEPTEMBER 7

20_____

1. _____
   _____
2. _____
   _____
3. _____
   _____

20_____

1. _____
   _____
2. _____
   _____
3. _____
   _____

20_____

1. _____
   _____
2. _____
   _____
3. _____
   _____

SEPTEMBER 8

20 _____

1. _____

   _____

2. _____

   _____

3. _____

   _____

20 _____

1. _____

   _____

2. _____

   _____

3. _____

   _____

20 _____

1. _____

   _____

2. _____

   _____

3. _____

   _____

SEPTEMBER 9

20_____

1. _____
_____

2. _____
_____

3. _____
_____

20_____

1. _____
_____

2. _____
_____

3. _____
_____

20_____

1. _____
_____

2. _____
_____

3. _____
_____

SEPTEMBER 10

) _____

1. _____
   _____
2. _____
   _____
3. _____
   _____

) _____

1. _____
   _____
2. _____
   _____
3. _____
   _____

) _____

1. _____
   _____
2. _____
   _____
3. _____
   _____

SEPTEMBER 11

20_____

1. _____
_____
2. _____
_____
3. _____
_____

20_____

1. _____
_____
2. _____
_____
3. _____
_____

20_____

1. _____
_____
2. _____
_____
3. _____
_____

O_____

1. _____

   _____

2. _____

   _____

3. _____

   _____

O_____

1. _____

   _____

2. _____

   _____

3. _____

   _____

O_____

1. _____

   _____

2. _____

   _____

3. _____

   _____

SEPTEMBER 13

20_____

1. _____

_____

2. _____

_____

3. _____

_____

20_____

1. _____

_____

2. _____

_____

3. _____

_____

20_____

1. _____

_____

2. _____

_____

3. _____

_____

SEPTEMBER 14

○ _____

1. _____

_____

2. _____

_____

3. _____

_____

○ _____

1. _____

_____

2. _____

_____

3. _____

_____

○ _____

1. _____

_____

2. _____

_____

3. _____

_____

SEPTEMBER 15

20_____

1. _____
   _____
2. _____
   _____
3. _____
   _____

20_____

1. _____
   _____
2. _____
   _____
3. _____
   _____

20_____

1. _____
   _____
2. _____
   _____
3. _____
   _____

SEPTEMBER 16

20 _____

1. _____
   _____
2. _____
   _____
3. _____
   _____

20 _____

1. _____
   _____
2. _____
   _____
3. _____
   _____

20 _____

1. _____
   _____
2. _____
   _____
3. _____
   _____

SEPTEMBER 17

20_____

1. _____
_____

2. _____
_____

3. _____
_____

20_____

1. _____
_____

2. _____
_____

3. _____
_____

20_____

1. _____
_____

2. _____
_____

3. _____
_____

SEPTEMBER 18

20_____

1. _____
   _____
2. _____
   _____
3. _____
   _____

20_____

1. _____
   _____
2. _____
   _____
3. _____
   _____

20_____

1. _____
   _____
2. _____
   _____
3. _____
   _____

SEPTEMBER 19

20_____

1. _____

_____

2. _____

_____

3. _____

_____

20_____

1. _____

_____

2. _____

_____

3. _____

_____

20_____

1. _____

_____

2. _____

_____

3. _____

_____

20_____

1. _____
   _____

2. _____
   _____

3. _____
   _____

20_____

1. _____
   _____

2. _____
   _____

3. _____
   _____

20_____

1. _____
   _____

2. _____
   _____

3. _____
   _____

SEPTEMBER 21

20_____

1. _____
   _____
2. _____
   _____
3. _____
   _____

20_____

1. _____
   _____
2. _____
   _____
3. _____
   _____

20_____

1. _____
   _____
2. _____
   _____
3. _____
   _____

SEPTEMBER 22

20_____

1. _____
   _____

2. _____
   _____

3. _____
   _____

20_____

1. _____
   _____

2. _____
   _____

3. _____
   _____

20_____

1. _____
   _____

2. _____
   _____

3. _____
   _____

SEPTEMBER 23

20_____

1. _____
   _____

2. _____
   _____

3. _____
   _____

20_____

1. _____
   _____

2. _____
   _____

3. _____
   _____

20_____

1. _____
   _____

2. _____
   _____

3. _____
   _____

SEPTEMBER 24

20_____

1. _____

_____

2. _____

_____

3. _____

_____

20_____

1. _____

_____

2. _____

_____

3. _____

_____

20_____

1. _____

_____

2. _____

_____

3. _____

_____

SEPTEMBER 25

20_____

1. _____
   _____
2. _____
   _____
3. _____
   _____

20_____

1. _____
   _____
2. _____
   _____
3. _____
   _____

20_____

1. _____
   _____
2. _____
   _____
3. _____
   _____

SEPTEMBER 26

20_____

1. _____
   _____

2. _____
   _____

3. _____
   _____

20_____

1. _____
   _____

2. _____
   _____

3. _____
   _____

20_____

1. _____
   _____

2. _____
   _____

3. _____
   _____

SEPTEMBER 27

20_____

1. _____
   _____

2. _____
   _____

3. _____
   _____

20_____

1. _____
   _____

2. _____
   _____

3. _____
   _____

20_____

1. _____
   _____

2. _____
   _____

3. _____
   _____

SEPTEMBER 28

20_____

1. _____
   _____
2. _____
   _____
3. _____
   _____

20_____

1. _____
   _____
2. _____
   _____
3. _____
   _____

20_____

1. _____
   _____
2. _____
   _____
3. _____
   _____

SEPTEMBER 29

20_____

   1. _____

   _____

   2. _____

   _____

   3. _____

   _____

20_____

   1. _____

   _____

   2. _____

   _____

   3. _____

   _____

20_____

   1. _____

   _____

   2. _____

   _____

   3. _____

   _____

SEPTEMBER 30

20_____

1. _____
_____

2. _____
_____

3. _____
_____

20_____

1. _____
_____

2. _____
_____

3. _____
_____

20_____

1. _____
_____

2. _____
_____

3. _____
_____

OCTOBER 1

20_____

1. _____
   _____
2. _____
   _____
3. _____
   _____

20_____

1. _____
   _____
2. _____
   _____
3. _____
   _____

20_____

1. _____
   _____
2. _____
   _____
3. _____
   _____

OCTOBER 2

20_____

1. _____

_____

2. _____

_____

3. _____

_____

20_____

1. _____

_____

2. _____

_____

3. _____

_____

20_____

1. _____

_____

2. _____

_____

3. _____

_____

OCTOBER 3

20_____

    1. _____

    _____

    2. _____

    _____

    3. _____

    _____

20_____

    1. _____

    _____

    2. _____

    _____

    3. _____

    _____

20_____

    1. _____

    _____

    2. _____

    _____

    3. _____

    _____

OCTOBER 4

20_____

1. _____
   _____
2. _____
   _____
3. _____
   _____

20_____

1. _____
   _____
2. _____
   _____
3. _____
   _____

20_____

1. _____
   _____
2. _____
   _____
3. _____
   _____

OCTOBER 5

20_____

   1. _____
     _____
   2. _____
     _____
   3. _____
     _____

20_____

   1. _____
     _____
   2. _____
     _____
   3. _____
     _____

20_____

   1. _____
     _____
   2. _____
     _____
   3. _____
     _____

OCTOBER 6

20_____

1. _____

_____

2. _____

_____

3. _____

_____

20_____

1. _____

_____

2. _____

_____

3. _____

_____

20_____

1. _____

_____

2. _____

_____

3. _____

_____

OCTOBER 7

20_____

   1. _____

     _____

   2. _____

     _____

   3. _____

     _____

20_____

   1. _____

     _____

   2. _____

     _____

   3. _____

     _____

20_____

   1. _____

     _____

   2. _____

     _____

   3. _____

     _____

OCTOBER 8

20_____

1. _____

_____

2. _____

_____

3. _____

_____

20_____

1. _____

_____

2. _____

_____

3. _____

_____

20_____

1. _____

_____

2. _____

_____

3. _____

_____

OCTOBER 9

20_____

    1. _____
    _____
    2. _____
    _____
    3. _____
    _____

20_____

    1. _____
    _____
    2. _____
    _____
    3. _____
    _____

20_____

    1. _____
    _____
    2. _____
    _____
    3. _____
    _____

OCTOBER 10

20_____

1. _____

_____

2. _____

_____

3. _____

_____

20_____

1. _____

_____

2. _____

_____

3. _____

_____

20_____

1. _____

_____

2. _____

_____

3. _____

_____

OCTOBER 11

20_____

1. _____
   _____

2. _____
   _____

3. _____
   _____

20_____

1. _____
   _____

2. _____
   _____

3. _____
   _____

20_____

1. _____
   _____

2. _____
   _____

3. _____
   _____

OCTOBER 12

20____

1. _____

_____

2. _____

_____

3. _____

_____

20____

1. _____

_____

2. _____

_____

3. _____

_____

20____

1. _____

_____

2. _____

_____

3. _____

_____

OCTOBER 13

20_____

   1. _____

     _____

   2. _____

     _____

   3. _____

     _____

20_____

   1. _____

     _____

   2. _____

     _____

   3. _____

     _____

20_____

   1. _____

     _____

   2. _____

     _____

   3. _____

     _____

OCTOBER 14

O _____

1. _____

_____

2. _____

_____

3. _____

_____

O _____

1. _____

_____

2. _____

_____

3. _____

_____

O _____

1. _____

_____

2. _____

_____

3. _____

_____

OCTOBER 15

20_____

1. _____
   _____
2. _____
   _____
3. _____
   _____

20_____

1. _____
   _____
2. _____
   _____
3. _____
   _____

20_____

1. _____
   _____
2. _____
   _____
3. _____
   _____

OCTOBER 16

20_____

   1. _____

      _____

   2. _____

      _____

   3. _____

      _____

20_____

   1. _____

      _____

   2. _____

      _____

   3. _____

      _____

20_____

   1. _____

      _____

   2. _____

      _____

   3. _____

      _____

OCTOBER 17

20_____

   1. _____
      _____

   2. _____
      _____

   3. _____
      _____

20_____

   1. _____
      _____

   2. _____
      _____

   3. _____
      _____

20_____

   1. _____
      _____

   2. _____
      _____

   3. _____
      _____

OCTOBER 18

20_____

1. _____
   _____
2. _____
   _____
3. _____
   _____

20_____

1. _____
   _____
2. _____
   _____
3. _____
   _____

20_____

1. _____
   _____
2. _____
   _____
3. _____
   _____

OCTOBER 19

20_____

   1. _____

   _____

   2. _____

   _____

   3. _____

   _____

20_____

   1. _____

   _____

   2. _____

   _____

   3. _____

   _____

20_____

   1. _____

   _____

   2. _____

   _____

   3. _____

   _____

OCTOBER 20

20_____

1. _____
_____

2. _____
_____

3. _____
_____

20_____

1. _____
_____

2. _____
_____

3. _____
_____

20_____

1. _____
_____

2. _____
_____

3. _____
_____

OCTOBER 21

20_____

   1. _____

   _____

   2. _____

   _____

   3. _____

   _____

20_____

   1. _____

   _____

   2. _____

   _____

   3. _____

   _____

20_____

   1. _____

   _____

   2. _____

   _____

   3. _____

   _____

OCTOBER 22

20_____

    1. _____

    _____

    2. _____

    _____

    3. _____

    _____

20_____

    1. _____

    _____

    2. _____

    _____

    3. _____

    _____

20_____

    1. _____

    _____

    2. _____

    _____

    3. _____

    _____

20_____

1. _____
_____

2. _____
_____

3. _____
_____

20_____

1. _____
_____

2. _____
_____

3. _____
_____

20_____

1. _____
_____

2. _____
_____

3. _____
_____

OCTOBER 24

20_____

1. _____

_____

2. _____

_____

3. _____

_____

20_____

1. _____

_____

2. _____

_____

3. _____

_____

20_____

1. _____

_____

2. _____

_____

3. _____

_____

OCTOBER 25

20_____

1. _____
_____

2. _____
_____

3. _____
_____

20_____

1. _____
_____

2. _____
_____

3. _____
_____

20_____

1. _____
_____

2. _____
_____

3. _____
_____

OCTOBER 26

20_____

1. _____
   _____

2. _____
   _____

3. _____
   _____

20_____

1. _____
   _____

2. _____
   _____

3. _____
   _____

20_____

1. _____
   _____

2. _____
   _____

3. _____
   _____

OCTOBER 27

20_____

1. _____
   _____
2. _____
   _____
3. _____
   _____

20_____

1. _____
   _____
2. _____
   _____
3. _____
   _____

20_____

1. _____
   _____
2. _____
   _____
3. _____
   _____

OCTOBER 28

20_____

   1. _____

     _____

   2. _____

     _____

   3. _____

     _____

20_____

   1. _____

     _____

   2. _____

     _____

   3. _____

     _____

20_____

   1. _____

     _____

   2. _____

     _____

   3. _____

     _____

OCTOBER 29

20_____

    1. _____

       _____

    2. _____

       _____

    3. _____

       _____

20_____

    1. _____

       _____

    2. _____

       _____

    3. _____

       _____

20_____

    1. _____

       _____

    2. _____

       _____

    3. _____

       _____

OCTOBER 30

20_____

1. _____

_____

2. _____

_____

3. _____

_____

20_____

1. _____

_____

2. _____

_____

3. _____

_____

20_____

1. _____

_____

2. _____

_____

3. _____

_____

OCTOBER 31

20_____

1. _____
   _____

2. _____
   _____

3. _____
   _____

20_____

1. _____
   _____

2. _____
   _____

3. _____
   _____

20_____

1. _____
   _____

2. _____
   _____

3. _____
   _____

NOVEMBER 1

20_____

1. _____

_____

2. _____

_____

3. _____

_____

20_____

1. _____

_____

2. _____

_____

3. _____

_____

20_____

1. _____

_____

2. _____

_____

3. _____

_____

NOVEMBER 2

20_____

    1. _____

    _____

    2. _____

    _____

    3. _____

    _____

20_____

    1. _____

    _____

    2. _____

    _____

    3. _____

    _____

20_____

    1. _____

    _____

    2. _____

    _____

    3. _____

    _____

NOVEMBER 3

20_____

  1. _____

  _____

  2. _____

  _____

  3. _____

  _____

20_____

  1. _____

  _____

  2. _____

  _____

  3. _____

  _____

20_____

  1. _____

  _____

  2. _____

  _____

  3. _____

  _____

NOVEMBER 4

20_____

1. _____
   _____
2. _____
   _____
3. _____
   _____

20_____

1. _____
   _____
2. _____
   _____
3. _____
   _____

20_____

1. _____
   _____
2. _____
   _____
3. _____
   _____

NOVEMBER 5

20_____

   1. _____

   _____

   2. _____

   _____

   3. _____

   _____

20_____

   1. _____

   _____

   2. _____

   _____

   3. _____

   _____

20_____

   1. _____

   _____

   2. _____

   _____

   3. _____

   _____

NOVEMBER 6

20_____

1. _____
   _____

2. _____
   _____

3. _____
   _____

20_____

1. _____
   _____

2. _____
   _____

3. _____
   _____

20_____

1. _____
   _____

2. _____
   _____

3. _____
   _____

NOVEMBER 7

20_____

1. _____

_____

2. _____

_____

3. _____

_____

20_____

1. _____

_____

2. _____

_____

3. _____

_____

20_____

1. _____

_____

2. _____

_____

3. _____

_____

NOVEMBER 8

20_____

1. _____
   _____
2. _____
   _____
3. _____
   _____

20_____

1. _____
   _____
2. _____
   _____
3. _____
   _____

20_____

1. _____
   _____
2. _____
   _____
3. _____
   _____

NOVEMBER 9

20_____

　　1. _____

　　　 _____

　　2. _____

　　　 _____

　　3. _____

　　　 _____

20_____

　　1. _____

　　　 _____

　　2. _____

　　　 _____

　　3. _____

　　　 _____

20_____

　　1. _____

　　　 _____

　　2. _____

　　　 _____

　　3. _____

　　　 _____

NOVEMBER 10

20_____

    1. _____

      _____

    2. _____

      _____

    3. _____

      _____

20_____

    1. _____

      _____

    2. _____

      _____

    3. _____

      _____

20_____

    1. _____

      _____

    2. _____

      _____

    3. _____

      _____

NOVEMBER 11

20_____

1. _____

_____

2. _____

_____

3. _____

_____

20_____

1. _____

_____

2. _____

_____

3. _____

_____

20_____

1. _____

_____

2. _____

_____

3. _____

_____

NOVEMBER 12

20_____

   1. _____

   _____

   2. _____

   _____

   3. _____

   _____

20_____

   1. _____

   _____

   2. _____

   _____

   3. _____

   _____

20_____

   1. _____

   _____

   2. _____

   _____

   3. _____

   _____

NOVEMBER 13

20_____

1. _____

_____

2. _____

_____

3. _____

_____

20_____

1. _____

_____

2. _____

_____

3. _____

_____

20_____

1. _____

_____

2. _____

_____

3. _____

_____

NOVEMBER 14

20_____

   1. _____

     _____

   2. _____

     _____

   3. _____

     _____

20_____

   1. _____

     _____

   2. _____

     _____

   3. _____

     _____

20_____

   1. _____

     _____

   2. _____

     _____

   3. _____

     _____

NOVEMBER 15

20_____

1. _____

_____

2. _____

_____

3. _____

_____

20_____

1. _____

_____

2. _____

_____

3. _____

_____

20_____

1. _____

_____

2. _____

_____

3. _____

_____

NOVEMBER 16

20_____

   1. _____

   _____

   2. _____

   _____

   3. _____

   _____

20_____

   1. _____

   _____

   2. _____

   _____

   3. _____

   _____

20_____

   1. _____

   _____

   2. _____

   _____

   3. _____

   _____

NOVEMBER 17

20_____

1. _____

_____

2. _____

_____

3. _____

_____

20_____

1. _____

_____

2. _____

_____

3. _____

_____

20_____

1. _____

_____

2. _____

_____

3. _____

_____

NOVEMBER 18

20_____

1. _____

_____

2. _____

_____

3. _____

_____

20_____

1. _____

_____

2. _____

_____

3. _____

_____

20_____

1. _____

_____

2. _____

_____

3. _____

_____

NOVEMBER 19

20_____

1. _____

_____

2. _____

_____

3. _____

_____

20_____

1. _____

_____

2. _____

_____

3. _____

_____

20_____

1. _____

_____

2. _____

_____

3. _____

_____

NOVEMBER 20

20_____

1. _____
   _____
2. _____
   _____
3. _____
   _____

20_____

1. _____
   _____
2. _____
   _____
3. _____
   _____

20_____

1. _____
   _____
2. _____
   _____
3. _____
   _____

NOVEMBER 21

20_____

1. _____
   _____
2. _____
   _____
3. _____
   _____

20_____

1. _____
   _____
2. _____
   _____
3. _____
   _____

20_____

1. _____
   _____
2. _____
   _____
3. _____
   _____

NOVEMBER 22

20_____

1. _____
_____

2. _____
_____

3. _____
_____

20_____

1. _____
_____

2. _____
_____

3. _____
_____

20_____

1. _____
_____

2. _____
_____

3. _____
_____

NOVEMBER 23

20_____

   1. _____

      _____

   2. _____

      _____

   3. _____

      _____

20_____

   1. _____

      _____

   2. _____

      _____

   3. _____

      _____

20_____

   1. _____

      _____

   2. _____

      _____

   3. _____

      _____

NOVEMBER 24

20_____

   1. _____

     _____

   2. _____

     _____

   3. _____

     _____

20_____

   1. _____

     _____

   2. _____

     _____

   3. _____

     _____

20_____

   1. _____

     _____

   2. _____

     _____

   3. _____

     _____

NOVEMBER 25

20_____

1. _____
   _____
2. _____
   _____
3. _____
   _____

20_____

1. _____
   _____
2. _____
   _____
3. _____
   _____

20_____

1. _____
   _____
2. _____
   _____
3. _____
   _____

NOVEMBER 26

20_____

1. _____

_____

2. _____

_____

3. _____

_____

20_____

1. _____

_____

2. _____

_____

3. _____

_____

20_____

1. _____

_____

2. _____

_____

3. _____

_____

NOVEMBER 27

20_____

1. _____
   _____
2. _____
   _____
3. _____
   _____

20_____

1. _____
   _____
2. _____
   _____
3. _____
   _____

20_____

1. _____
   _____
2. _____
   _____
3. _____
   _____

NOVEMBER 28

20_____

1. _____
_____
2. _____
_____
3. _____
_____

20_____

1. _____
_____
2. _____
_____
3. _____
_____

20_____

1. _____
_____
2. _____
_____
3. _____
_____

NOVEMBER 29

20_____

1. _____
   _____

2. _____
   _____

3. _____
   _____

20_____

1. _____
   _____

2. _____
   _____

3. _____
   _____

20_____

1. _____
   _____

2. _____
   _____

3. _____
   _____

NOVEMBER 30

20_____

1. _____
   _____

2. _____
   _____

3. _____
   _____

20_____

1. _____
   _____

2. _____
   _____

3. _____
   _____

20_____

1. _____
   _____

2. _____
   _____

3. _____
   _____

DECEMBER 1

20_____

1. _____
   _____
2. _____
   _____
3. _____
   _____

20_____

1. _____
   _____
2. _____
   _____
3. _____
   _____

20_____

1. _____
   _____
2. _____
   _____
3. _____
   _____

DECEMBER 2

20_____

   1. _____

      _____

   2. _____

      _____

   3. _____

      _____

20_____

   1. _____

      _____

   2. _____

      _____

   3. _____

      _____

20_____

   1. _____

      _____

   2. _____

      _____

   3. _____

      _____

DECEMBER 3

20_____

1. _____
   _____

2. _____
   _____

3. _____
   _____

20_____

1. _____
   _____

2. _____
   _____

3. _____
   _____

20_____

1. _____
   _____

2. _____
   _____

3. _____
   _____

DECEMBER 4

20_____

1. _____
_____
2. _____
_____
3. _____
_____

20_____

1. _____
_____
2. _____
_____
3. _____
_____

20_____

1. _____
_____
2. _____
_____
3. _____
_____

DECEMBER 5

20_____

1. _____

_____

2. _____

_____

3. _____

_____

20_____

1. _____

_____

2. _____

_____

3. _____

_____

20_____

1. _____

_____

2. _____

_____

3. _____

_____

DECEMBER 6

20_____

   1. _____

     _____

   2. _____

     _____

   3. _____

     _____

20_____

   1. _____

     _____

   2. _____

     _____

   3. _____

     _____

20_____

   1. _____

     _____

   2. _____

     _____

   3. _____

     _____

DECEMBER 7

20_____

1. _____

_____

2. _____

_____

3. _____

_____

20_____

1. _____

_____

2. _____

_____

3. _____

_____

20_____

1. _____

_____

2. _____

_____

3. _____

_____

DECEMBER 8

20_____

1. _____
   _____
2. _____
   _____
3. _____
   _____

20_____

1. _____
   _____
2. _____
   _____
3. _____
   _____

20_____

1. _____
   _____
2. _____
   _____
3. _____
   _____

DECEMBER 9

20_____

1. _____
   _____
2. _____
   _____
3. _____
   _____

20_____

1. _____
   _____
2. _____
   _____
3. _____
   _____

20_____

1. _____
   _____
2. _____
   _____
3. _____
   _____

DECEMBER 10

20_____

1. _____
_____
2. _____
_____
3. _____
_____

20_____

1. _____
_____
2. _____
_____
3. _____
_____

20_____

1. _____
_____
2. _____
_____
3. _____
_____

DECEMBER 11

20_____

    1. _____

    _____

    2. _____

    _____

    3. _____

    _____

20_____

    1. _____

    _____

    2. _____

    _____

    3. _____

    _____

20_____

    1. _____

    _____

    2. _____

    _____

    3. _____

    _____

DECEMBER 12

20_____

1. _____

   _____

2. _____

   _____

3. _____

   _____

20_____

1. _____

   _____

2. _____

   _____

3. _____

   _____

20_____

1. _____

   _____

2. _____

   _____

3. _____

   _____

DECEMBER 13

20_____

   1. _____

     _____

   2. _____

     _____

   3. _____

     _____

20_____

   1. _____

     _____

   2. _____

     _____

   3. _____

     _____

20_____

   1. _____

     _____

   2. _____

     _____

   3. _____

     _____

DECEMBER 14

20_____

1. _____
   _____
2. _____
   _____
3. _____
   _____

20_____

1. _____
   _____
2. _____
   _____
3. _____
   _____

20_____

1. _____
   _____
2. _____
   _____
3. _____
   _____

DECEMBER 15

20_____

1. _____
   _____
2. _____
   _____
3. _____
   _____

20_____

1. _____
   _____
2. _____
   _____
3. _____
   _____

20_____

1. _____
   _____
2. _____
   _____
3. _____
   _____

DECEMBER 16

20_____

   1. _____

     _____

   2. _____

     _____

   3. _____

     _____

20_____

   1. _____

     _____

   2. _____

     _____

   3. _____

     _____

20_____

   1. _____

     _____

   2. _____

     _____

   3. _____

     _____

DECEMBER 17

20_____

1. _____
   _____

2. _____
   _____

3. _____
   _____

20_____

1. _____
   _____

2. _____
   _____

3. _____
   _____

20_____

1. _____
   _____

2. _____
   _____

3. _____
   _____

DECEMBER 18

20_____

1. _____
   _____

2. _____
   _____

3. _____
   _____

20_____

1. _____
   _____

2. _____
   _____

3. _____
   _____

20_____

1. _____
   _____

2. _____
   _____

3. _____
   _____

DECEMBER 19

20_____

   1. _____

   _____

   2. _____

   _____

   3. _____

   _____

20_____

   1. _____

   _____

   2. _____

   _____

   3. _____

   _____

20_____

   1. _____

   _____

   2. _____

   _____

   3. _____

   _____

DECEMBER 20

20_____

1. _____
   _____

2. _____
   _____

3. _____
   _____

20_____

1. _____
   _____

2. _____
   _____

3. _____
   _____

20_____

1. _____
   _____

2. _____
   _____

3. _____
   _____

DECEMBER 21

20_____

1. _____
_____
2. _____
_____
3. _____
_____

20_____

1. _____
_____
2. _____
_____
3. _____
_____

20_____

1. _____
_____
2. _____
_____
3. _____
_____

DECEMBER 22

20_____

1. _____
   _____

2. _____
   _____

3. _____
   _____

20_____

1. _____
   _____

2. _____
   _____

3. _____
   _____

20_____

1. _____
   _____

2. _____
   _____

3. _____
   _____

DECEMBER 23

20_____

   1. _____

   _____

   2. _____

   _____

   3. _____

   _____

20_____

   1. _____

   _____

   2. _____

   _____

   3. _____

   _____

20_____

   1. _____

   _____

   2. _____

   _____

   3. _____

   _____

DECEMBER 24

20_____

1. _____
_____

2. _____
_____

3. _____
_____

20_____

1. _____
_____

2. _____
_____

3. _____
_____

20_____

1. _____
_____

2. _____
_____

3. _____
_____

DECEMBER 25

20_____

   1. _____

     _____

   2. _____

     _____

   3. _____

     _____

20_____

   1. _____

     _____

   2. _____

     _____

   3. _____

     _____

20_____

   1. _____

     _____

   2. _____

     _____

   3. _____

     _____

DECEMBER 26

20_____

1. _____
   _____

2. _____
   _____

3. _____
   _____

20_____

1. _____
   _____

2. _____
   _____

3. _____
   _____

20_____

1. _____
   _____

2. _____
   _____

3. _____
   _____

DECEMBER 27

20_____

   1. _____

     _____

   2. _____

     _____

   3. _____

     _____

20_____

   1. _____

     _____

   2. _____

     _____

   3. _____

     _____

20_____

   1. _____

     _____

   2. _____

     _____

   3. _____

     _____

DECEMBER 28

20_____

1. _____
   _____

2. _____
   _____

3. _____
   _____

20_____

1. _____
   _____

2. _____
   _____

3. _____
   _____

20_____

1. _____
   _____

2. _____
   _____

3. _____
   _____

DECEMBER 29

20_____

1. _____
   _____
2. _____
   _____
3. _____
   _____

20_____

1. _____
   _____
2. _____
   _____
3. _____
   _____

20_____

1. _____
   _____
2. _____
   _____
3. _____
   _____

DECEMBER 30

20_____

1. _____
   _____
2. _____
   _____
3. _____
   _____

20_____

1. _____
   _____
2. _____
   _____
3. _____
   _____

20_____

1. _____
   _____
2. _____
   _____
3. _____
   _____

DECEMBER 31

20_____

1. _____
   _____

2. _____
   _____

3. _____
   _____

20_____

1. _____
   _____

2. _____
   _____

3. _____
   _____

20_____

1. _____
   _____

2. _____
   _____

3. _____
   _____

Published in the United States by Clarkson Potter/Publishers, an imprint of
Random House, a division of Penguin Random House LLC, New York.
clarksonpotter.com

CLARKSON POTTER is a trademark and POTTER with colophon is a
registered trademark of Penguin Random House LLC.

ISBN 978-0-593-13974-5

Printed in China
Design by Annalisa Sheldahl
10 9 8 7 6 5 4 3 2 1
First Edition